Te[illegible]ums

A BEGINNER'S GUIDE

Manos Kanellos

This book is dedicated to my children, Andreas and Alexia.

Published in 2024 by Kamara Productions, Hanwell, W7 3AF, UK.
ISBN 978-1-91646-213-7
British Library Cataloguing in Publication Data
A catalogue record for this book is available from the British Library.

Text: Manos Kanellos
Design, typesetting and page layout: Steve Balcombe
Project and production management: Manos Kanellos

Printed and bound in Great Britain by Carly Press.

MIX
Paper from responsible sources
FSC® C015170

Contents

Introduction

What is a terrarium?

The word terrarium comes from the Latin 'terra' (earth) and '-arium' (a place or receptacle), i.e., a place for earth.

A terrarium is a collection of small or miniature plants, grown in a transparent glass container with no drainage. This lack of drainage is what makes terrariums special in terms of putting them together and caring for them. A terrarium is your own miniature indoor garden that can provide lots of enjoyment and year-round interest.

You can use almost any container from glass to acrylic, and a wide range of plants such as cacti, succulents, tropical foliage plants or even air plants. You can put them together in whatever way you fancy to create a unique display. This book aims to explain in detail how to make a terrarium and how to look after it, so you can enjoy it with minimum effort. There are plenty of ideas and inspiration to create your own, unique piece of horticultural art.

History of terrariums

The first terrarium was accidentally developed by Dr Nathanial Bagshaw Ward in 1829, in south London. Ward was fascinated by insects, particularly moths and caterpillars, which he kept in jars in his back yard. When he found a fern seedling growing in a closed jar, it got him thinking that many humidity loving plants could exist in a contained environment, so he developed the concept for what became known as the 'Wardian Case'. The principal use of the Wardian case was the transportation of tropical plants which had previously proved extremely difficult to keep alive over long journeys.

The general idea of a Wardian Case is the same as the modern-day closed terrarium.

Ward's invention would see many amendments over the following decades, with containers being made out of metal instead of wood, and some with open lids. In the homes of the elite in the UK and Europe, Wardian Cases became a popular fashion statement. Owning a domestic Wardian Case with rare plants such as orchids and ferns would illustrate the owner's wealth and knowledge of horticulture.

It is said that there is no park in London without a plant that travelled in Dr Ward's Case.

An open terrarium with a mixture of cacti and succulents, put together using the card technique (see p46). The interplay of plants and vertical stones creates an interesting, desert themed display.

Types of modern terrariums

Today we can distinguish between them according to the type of container used: closed, partially open or fully open.

Closed terrariums

A closed terrarium with a cork lid.

These are often called bottle gardens and have a lid which allows humidity to build up on the inside, and makes them almost self-sufficient in terms of watering. The plants will absorb the moisture through the roots, before transpiring it from the leaves, thus re-entering the enclosed atmosphere. The moisture will then build up until droplets form on the side of the glass, which eventually trickle down into the soil to start the process all over again. Closed terrariums are great for plants which thrive in high humidity, but unsuitable for plants such as cacti or succulents which do not do well in high humidity.

Partially open terrariums

These are containers with an opening on top or the side, which make the humidity inside the container a little higher than outside.

Most plants will thrive in a partially open terrarium. However, cacti and succulents need a good-sized opening to promote air circulation. The larger the opening, the better the air circulation, and the more suitable the container is for cacti or succulents.

Open terrariums

These have a fully open top and they are suitable for any plant. Open terrariums can be treated as glorified pots, and can be placed in as much light as the plants used in the terrarium require. Although some plants prefer the high humidity of a closed terrarium, they could also do well in an open terrarium, especially if sprayed with water regularly.

An open terrarium with cacti and succulents in a half bowl.

A partially open terrarium in the shape of a large bottle, with an opening on the front. A parlour palm and a croton at the back give the display height and colour. A whiteish nerve plant and a moon valley plant add more colour; a mini dragon tree in the middle, protruding forwards, adds depth.

A partially open terrarium with one plant (missionary plant), and sphagnum moss as ground cover.

An open terrarium with a single architectural succulent, and light-coloured grit for contrast. Often, less is more.

An open terrarium with tropical foliage plants. A layer of small grade white grit offers contrast.

What you need to make a terrarium

To make your own terrarium, you will need a glass container, clay pebbles (or large gravel), activated carbon, repotting mix and some plants of your choice that are suitable for that type of terrarium. Optionally, you can use some dried moss or a piece of permeable membrane, decorative grit and any suitable decorations of your choice.

TIP: When buying a ready-made terrarium, examine it closely. Does it have a drainage layer? If it does, it is easier to look after it. Does it contain plants with similar light requirements? If not, it is unlikely to succeed.

Glass container

There are plenty of containers from which to choose, so it really comes down to personal choice and style. You can buy some top-quality statement glass, or you can use an old glass jar you have had for years. You can use almost anything: jars, glass vases, fishbowls, half bowls, glass globes, coffee jars (with a lid or not), cylinders, apothecary jars, vintage Wardian cases, hanging containers, even giant wine glasses or footed fruit bowls!

In terms of material, clear glass is the most common and readily available. It is also easy to find green tinted glass. It may be more decorative, but green (or blue or brownish) tinted glass will reduce the amount of light the plants receive, so you need to take this into account when selecting plants, and when considering where to place the terrarium. It will also affect the way you view the plants inside the terrarium; maybe choose plants with variegated or colourful leaves for a better effect.

Terrariums can be very simple. An open terrarium made from a coffee jar and a single plant (nerve plant).

TIP: When choosing a glass container, consider the plants you want to use, the available depth for planting and the location you want to place it in.

Acrylic (high quality plastic) containers are also an option. They come in various shapes (triangular or pyramid are very common), they tend to cost less and are less likely to break, hence safer around children and animals. However, they tend to scratch more easily.

Whatever the material, and irrespective of whether the container is to be used as an open or closed terrarium, you also need to consider its opening. Containers with a small opening, which you cannot fit your hand in, will be significantly more difficult to plant up and will restrict the plants you can use as they will need to be very small. If the opening is too small to put your hand in, you will need some tools for working inside your terrarium.

One of the most important factors to take into account when choosing a container is depth: is it deep enough to accommodate a good drainage layer along with a decent layer of potting mix to accommodate the plants? Although shallow containers can be used for air plant terrariums, or very small plants, a minimum depth of 5 cm is required, with 6 to 8 cm ideal for planting.

Clay pebbles

These will be used to create a drainage layer at the bottom of the container. The function of this layer is to ensure that excess water doesn't stay in the soil, which can cause root rot.

A variety of materials can be used for the drainage layer, but large size/grade materials (10 mm to 20 mm) such as clay pebbles, gravel, marbles or small stones work best. Clay pebbles (also known as hydroleca, or simply 'lecca') are ideal as they can absorb water, so they reduce the risk of algal growth at the bottom of the container. You can also use their colour as an indicator of when the terrarium needs watering. When they have a dark brown colour, they are full of moisture; when they are light brown it is time to consider watering.

The drainage layer should be about half the depth of the potting mix layer. For example, if the glass container has 7 cm available depth for planting, the drainage layer could be about 2 cm, the potting mix layer about 4 cm, with 0.5 cm for the decorative layer.

Although it is possible to make a terrarium without a drainage layer, its maintenance would be tricky and you run a high risk of overwatering which can lead to plant death.

Opposite:
A small, open terrarium with cacti, in an acrylic container. A mixture of cacti, succulents and slates creates an interesting display.

A tiny, closed terrarium with a very small peace lily. It lacks a drainage layer, so needs extra care with watering.

Separation layer

Optionally, you could add a thin barrier between the drainage layer and the potting mix to ensure that the soil does not get mixed with the drainage layer. A divider will create a clear, distinct layer of separation.

The divider could be a thin permeable membrane such as a coffee filter, strong paper, or ideally a piece of weed control membrane, which allows water through but not particles. Cut properly in the shape of the container it would be invisible.

Alternatively (or additionally on top of the membrane) you can use a layer of dried moss, or sphagnum moss. It is very decorative and will also help absorb any excess moisture. The moss layer will add a pretty colour and texture as the middle layer of your terrarium, making it more visually attractive.

Separation membrane placed on the drainage layer

A closed terrarium with a mini dragon tree for height, and a few nerve plants for colour. A layer of dried moss between the drainage layer and the potting mix adds interest and variation.

An open terrarium with a flowering kalanchoe and contrasting grit layers. When using different types of grit, the usual way is for the larger size to go at the bottom and the smaller size at the top, but it can often work the other way round.

Less is more. A simple, open terrarium with a layer of 'baby tears'.
The Buddha adds interest and a sense of tranquillity.

Activated carbon

Activated carbon (or charcoal) is a form of carbon that is processed so that it has more pores. This creates a larger surface area with which to filter contaminants around it. It is a fine, odourless, black, gritty material which is sometimes used in emergency rooms to treat overdoses due to its toxin-absorbing properties. It is similar to what is inside drinking water filter cartridges.

Only a few teaspoonfuls are required above the drainage layer, or on top of the separation membrane or layer of moss if you opt for it. It will significantly improve the overall growing conditions and help fight off bacterial and fungi growth, reducing the chance of diseases.

Potting mix

TIP: Mix one teaspoonful of activated carbon per litre of potting mix to further minimise the risk of any fungal or bacterial growth in the terrarium.

It is best to use a specialist peat-free compost for terrariums, but houseplant-labelled potting mixes, or a cactus mix if you are making a desert terrarium, are good too. If you don't plan to use a top dressing (see page 22), it is advisable to use a compost that does not contain perlite or vermiculite, as this can rise to the surface and stick to the leaves of the plants.

If the potting mix is dry, it is a good idea to wet it before use (but do not add so much water that it becomes sloppy). You need to add enough potting mix so that it is deep enough for the plants to root into. Generally, this layer needs to be about 3–4 cm, but it can be more if the container has enough depth.

Plants

These are the stars of the show! When selecting plants for your terrarium, there are a few things you should keep in mind.

Firstly, consider the location and light and decide on the type of terrarium you want. If the location does not receive any direct sunlight you can go for any type of terrarium and it is bright enough a terrarium with cacti or succulents is also an option.

If you want a terrarium for a location that receives a couple of hours of direct sunlight throughout the year (such as an east or west facing windowsill), then an open terrarium with cacti or succulents would be the safest option.

Secondly, remember to combine plants with similar light, temperature and moisture requirements: a display which mixes cacti and ferns will not last very long!

TIP: If you mix cacti and succulents, the succulents may take over the display as they tend to grow much faster than cacti.

Thirdly, bear in mind the size of the glass container you want, and choose plants that are of an appropriate size. Ideally, you won't want any leaves touching the sides of your container. In closed terrariums, condensation will be trapped between the leaves and the glass, and the leaves may turn black due to sitting in water. Additionally, leaves touching the glass will make the terrarium look cramped (though perhaps this is the exact style you like).

If you choose fast growing plants like the polka dot plant or spider plants, you will get the 'overgrown jungle' effect quickly, whereas if you opt for plants that grow slowly like cacti (or in terms of foliage plants something like crotons or dragon trees) your terrarium will maintain the same look for many months. See "Plants for terrariums" on page 68 for suggested plants.

Mini houseplants suitable for terrariums, clockwise from left:

- *Variegated peperomia (Peperomia caperata)*
- *Panda plant (Kalanchoe tomentosa)*
- *Parlour palm (Chamaedorea elegans)*
- *Peace lily (Spathiphyllum)*
- *String of pearls (Curio rowleyanus, syn. Senecio rowleyanus)*
- *White variegated polka dot plant (Hypoestes phyllostachya)*
- *Pink nerve plant (Fittonia albivenis 'Forest Flame' Red)*

A collection of miniature plants suitable for terrariums, clockwise from rear left:

- *Peperomia (Peperomia caperata 'Rosso')*
- *Mini green dragon tree (Dracaena reflexa)*
- *Mini variegated dragon tree (Dracaena fragrans)*
- *Red polka dot plant (Hypoestes phyllostachya)*
- *Variegated dracaena (Dracaena marginata)*
- *White polka dot plant (Hypoestes phyllostachya)*
- *Green inch plant (Tradescantia zebrina)*
- *Peperomia (Peperomia verticillata 'Red Log')*
- *Mini valley plant (Peperomia rotundifolia)*

Preparing the plants

Splitting

Most plants can be divided or split before use, as even the mini plants sold specifically for terrariums are too big sometimes. Using plants as they are would only allow for one or two plants in an average glass container and would create a 'full' plant display immediately – which is not always a bad thing. But splitting plants enables you to use many different plants, even in small containers, creating a more diverse display.

Many plants sold for terrariums can be easily split into many plants with minimum root disturbance. Nerve plants, begonias, peperomias and peace lilies are examples of easy-to-split plants. Not all plants can be split – if in doubt ask the nursery or garden centre.

Some plants, such as nerve plants (but not the very similar polka dot plant), are a collection of rooted cuttings. They can be easily split, with minimum root disturbance.

Peace lilies can easily be split into smaller plants. Splitting plants allows for the use of a variety of different plants, without it looking overcrowded.

A polka dot plant is pinched before being planted. Pinching plants is a good way to ensure they remain compact and do not take over the display.

Pinching

Pinching, also known as tipping, is a pruning method which removes the top two leaves of the plants to encourage branching and to create more compact plants. For terrariums it prevents the display getting overgrown too quickly. Most plants can be pinched, but plants that won't tolerate being pinched include cacti, ferns, palms and peace lilies.

TIP: Pinch the plants before you place them in the terrarium, as it would be considerably more difficult to do so once inside.

Some succulents will also benefit from pinching before use, and will respond with compact, bushy growth.

Top dressing

After all your plants are arranged in the glass, you can top dress the terrarium with a layer of decorative material. You can use grit, sand, brightly coloured or horticultural sand, aquarium gravel, dried moss, river pebbles, crushed marble, glitter or even coloured glass chips. Although not essential, such a layer can add contrast, colour and layers of visual interest. It can be an important design element. Top dressing creates a neat look and prevents moisture from escaping an open terrarium, much like mulch in the garden. Small sized, light-coloured grit works best, but it is purely down to personal taste.

TIP: Wash the grit or stones before use to prevent dust particles washing into the potting mix.

Additionally, decorations can brighten up a terrarium and give it a personal touch. Again, it comes down to personal taste. You can use almost anything: stones, small slates, seashells, fossils, driftwood, toy animal features, fairy garden miniatures etc. Anything organic (pine cones, bark pieces etc) should be thoroughly cleaned and disinfected before use. Organic ornaments are best avoided in closed terrariums as they can attract mould.

Alternatively, after all the plants are arranged you can use ground-covering plants (like baby tears or Irish moss) to create a jungle or tropical forest display, perhaps with some slate-coloured stones for texture.

TIP: If you use stones on top of the grit or sand, bury them a little for a more natural look.

An open terrarium with a variegated peperomia and a croton for height, and a begonia and a mini philodendron at the front. Two vertical slabs frame the display which is decorated with a layer of decorative crushed shells. Crushed shells should be washed well before use, to avoid excessive calcium levels in the soil.

An open terrarium with a mixture of plants and a layer of different sizes of cork chippings and a decorative piece of cork at the back for a natural look.

TIP: You can use more than one type or size of grit to add variety and interest. Maybe in a yin-yang shape, or create a corridor, or sections of different complementary materials.

Two open terrariums with similar plant arrangements – a parlour palm for height and nerve plants for colour – but with a very different look due to the top dressing, with white grit (left) and decorative silver sand (below).

An open terrarium in an old-fashioned milk jar. The varying level of the decorative grit offers added interest.

An open terrarium with two levels of soil, separated by decorative stones. The two different decorative grits – one at the back and one in front – provide contrast.

Tools

Your best tools for making a terrarium are your hands, but if you cannot get your hand into the terrarium you will need to use small tools to position the items.

You can buy specialised terrarium tools which tend to be miniature versions of garden tools made from stainless steel, metal, or plastic. Alternatively, you can use a variety of tools from your kitchen. Plastic kitchen funnels, paper funnels, chopsticks, tongs, bamboo pieces, pastry brushes with long handles, as well as long forks, spoons, or pieces of strong malleable wire all work well.

TIP: Chopsticks or bamboo skewers can be used to move anything that needs moving within the terrarium.

Funnels can be very useful for pouring in soil or sand so that it does not adhere to the glass. A long-handled brush can be used to remove sand from any plant, along with a pair of sturdy tongs to place plants (especially cacti) and decorations in the terrarium.

Putting the terrarium together

Firstly, create a drainage layer, then (optionally) add a separation layer, followed by the carbon and the soil.

TIP: Use BBQ tongs or wear protective gloves to protect yourself from cactus spines. Alternatively, cover them with paper or bubble wrap for easier handling.

Next, prepare the plants. Take them out of their pots and remove any soil you can without disturbing the roots. Cacti and succulents are best re-potted on the dry side, but most other plants are best planted after they have been watered the day before. Split any plants you want to, so you can accommodate a bigger variety in the terrarium. Pinch the ones that you can so you will get bushy, compact growth.

TIP: All plants should be planted to the level they were in their pots. Burying them in the compost runs the risk of diseases, especially for cacti and succulents.

Play around with the placement of your plants outside the glass to see how they look best together. Move them around until they complement each other. Place the plants inside the container before you start to do a final check. For each plant dig a small hole into the soil to accommodate its root ball. Nestle the plant into the soil – do not worry about making it very sturdy; the decorative grit will help secure plants in their position. If you are not using decorative grit, you can always add some compost on top when all the plants are in place.

Regarding planting, it is easier to work your way from the back to the front of your terrarium. It is also important not to press down the compost – compaction will reduce the drainage of the mix and make rooting harder for the plants. Watering will ensure good contact between the roots and the potting mix.

Finally, add a layer of decorative grit if you wish. A good technique is to pour the grit towards the glass (with your hand or a large spoon) and use a chopstick to move it towards and between the plants.

Design principles

When putting the plant display together, as long as the plants all have similar requirements with regard to growing conditions, it is all a matter of personal taste. There are, however, a few general principles worth considering:

- You need to consider how the terrarium will be displayed. Will it have a front and back? Or will it be seen from every angle, like on a table? This will determine where the taller plants should go, i.e. at the back or at the centre.
- Try to create a layered effect with two or three layers of plants of different heights, just as you would do with a normal border in the garden. By placing the small plants at the front and the tall ones at the back, you will create a cascading effect where the eye can wander from the bottom of the display to the taller plants at the back.

- Cacti and succulents can easily be arranged with stones or vertical slates for a more interesting, desert-like effect. Mixing foliage plants and slates or stones can also be highly complementary and decorative.

Watering

If you used well-watered plants, it is best not to water the terrarium for about a week or so. This gives plants a chance to recover from being handled and to heal any damage done to their roots. When you water, do so slowly, and only around the plants, until they start spreading their roots. Resist the urge to water. Check your display weekly for signs of growth. You know your plants are well established when you can see the first roots reaching the glass.

TIP: Do not confuse loving your terrarium with watering your terrarium!

Putting a terrarium together

❶ *Add 2–3 cm of clay pebbles for the drainage layer.*

❷ *Add activated carbon on top of the clay pebbles.*

❸ *Add a layer (approx. 4 cm) of potting mix.*

❹ *Add the plants, along with a layer of small grade decorative grit.*

This container comes with a cork lid, so there is an option to have it as a partially open or closed terrarium. The plants are selected to be suitable for both.

Putting a terrarium together – an alternative version

❶ *Add small grade grit to the bottom of the fish bowl for the drainage layer.*

❷ *Add some activated carbon to minimise fungal and bacterial growth.*

❸ *Add wet sphagnum moss around the activated carbon. The moss layer is mostly for visual interest, and is not meant to work as a separation layer (hence why the carbon is added first).*

❹ *Add potting mix (specifically for terrariums) to good depth, and sprinkle some carbon over it.*

❺ *After experimenting with different combinations, place the plants in the best position. A combination of variegated and green plants creates interest and variation.*

❻ *A layer of large decorative gravel picks up the colour from the variegated dragon tree (tallest plant), and adds contrast and further interest.*

Some glass containers have an LED light which can be used to brighten the display in the dark. The LED light is unlikely to be beneficial for plant growth, but as it is cool it will not harm the plants.

A partially open terrarium in the shape of an apple. A mini peace lily at the back provides height, a couple of nerve plants add colour, and a mini Inch plant (Tradescantia) adds a third layer of interest. Light coloured, small grade grit offers contrast with the colourful plants.

An open terrarium with succulents. Vertical slates and stones provide an interesting background to the plants.

Caring for a terrarium

Temperature

The ideal temperature for a terrarium is between 16° and 25°C, which is the average temperature range in a centrally-heated house. If the temperature regularly falls below 12°C it can harm plants, and may lead to black markings on the leaf edges, poor growth or diseases. Very high temperatures, for long intervals, will need to be accompanied by high humidity (regular misting for open terrariums) and correct watering. High temperatures, especially when accompanied by inadequate light, will lead to leggy plants.

A partially open terrarium in the shape of a fishbowl. It is designed to be viewed from any angle, with a palm at its centre surrounded by nerve plants of various colours. The white grit adds interest and contrast.

Light

The most important factor for success with terrariums, just as for all houseplants, is location; which in turn determines the amount of light the plants will receive. The best location for your terrarium largely depends on whether it is an open, partially open or a closed terrarium, and what plants it contains, i.e. foliage plants or cacti/succulents.

TIP: If you cannot read a newspaper in a position, then it is not ideal for a terrarium (or for most common houseplants)

The plants must be right for the type of terrarium, and the terrarium should be placed in a suitable location. The location will determine which container and plants you can use, although it can of course be the other way round: you can choose a container and appropriate plants and place it in a suitable location.

It is relatively simple. Like most houseplants, terrariums should be placed in the brightest possible place (but not in direct sunlight) – except for terrariums with cacti or succulents. These could be placed in direct sunlight i.e., a windowsill during winter (November to February). Plenty of light will ensure they achieve maximum and compact growth. Direct sunlight in spring or summer, however, is likely to cause scorching.

Closed terrariums should never be placed in direct sunlight as the container will transform into an oven. A bright position, will ensure good growth and compact plants which is especially important during the winter months due to the overall low light levels. If the closed terrarium contains plants requiring low light (such as ferns), a north facing room could be good enough.

The key to terrarium success is the right combination of terrarium type, plants and location. It is a three-way interaction which, if you get right (accompanied by correct watering), is your assurance of success.

An open terrarium with a single asparagus fern at the back. Layers of colourful grit (of varied grades) and glass chippings add contrast and interest. Ideal for 'low light' such as a north facing room.

Watering

Overwatering i.e. too much water in one go, or watering too frequently, is the most common reason that terrariums and houseplants fail.

What kind of water?

As with all houseplants, it is best to use rain water or soft water, which do not contain any chemicals or salts. You can use water from filter jugs, but do not use water from domestic water softeners as these may use salts to soften the water.

Hard water is unlikely to harm plants, but it makes it difficult for them to thrive, especially in the long term, as salts accumulate. Also, it is likely to result in salt stains on the glass.

How often to water

The frequency of watering depends on a number of factors, such as:

- the type of terrarium – closed terrariums will need much less watering than open ones as water 'circulates' within the closed container;
- the type of plants in the terrarium – desert displays will need much less watering than foliage ones, for example
- the amount of sunlight your terrarium receives and the overall room temperature – terrariums in brighter, warmer rooms (or in the summer) will need more regular watering that terrariums in north-facing rooms, or in less bright conditions.

As a rule of thumb, allow the top third of the soil to dry out in between waterings, keeping in mind potential waterlogging in the base.

TIP: As terrariums lack drainage, only water when necessary. If in doubt, don't water.

There are two more indicators you can use for watering: the colour of the soil, and the colour of the clay pebbles if you have used them as the drainage layer. When wet, the compost will be dark brown, and as it dries, it'll become lighter in colour. Similarly, when the clay pebbles are light brown and it is dry at the bottom of the drainage layer, it is time to consider watering.

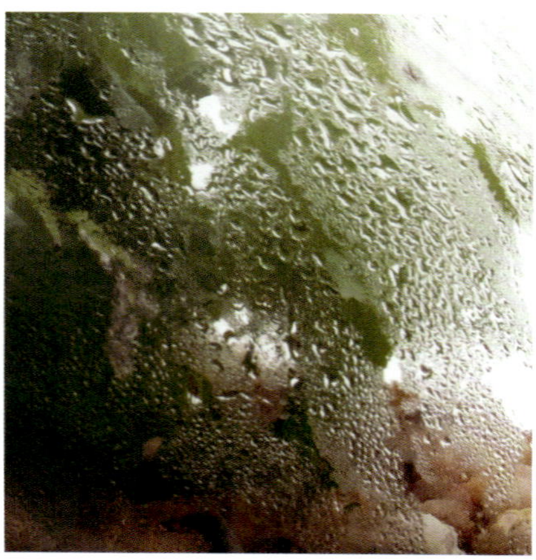

Sometimes you may see droplets of water on the glass surface inside your closed terrarium, especially after watering. If so, open the container for a few hours. In any case, it is a good practise to open the container for a few hours after watering to allow fresh air inside the terrarium which will help with plant growth.

How to water

It is best to water very slowly so the water spreads around the substrate, and doesn't go straight into the drainage layer. If possible, use a large tablespoon, the stream mode of a mister, or a pipette, and water only around the base of the plants to avoid overwatering.

For terrariums with cacti or succulents, keep the soil on the dry side by allowing it to dry well between waterings. This will significantly reduce the risk of any disease.

TIP: Always use tepid water when watering your plants. This hydrates much better and will eliminate any risk of shock to the plant.

Humidity

Similar to all houseplants, open terrariums with foliage plants (only) will benefit from regular spraying. Use rain water or soft water to prevent the build-up of salts within the terrarium, or use a foliar feed such as Houseplant Myst to provide some extra nutrients.

A terrarium with ferns, nerve plants and an inch plant. The fern at the back provides height. Nerve plants add colour and decorative green grit provides a 'grass effect'. It works well as either an open terrarium, or as a closed one with the glass lid on.

Feeding

Overall, your terrarium will need less nutrients than normal house plants, as plants in these displays tend to grow more slowly. Most repotting mixes for terrariums contain nutrients for about two to three months, so there is no need to feed during this period.

For terrariums with foliage plants, use a good quality houseplant feed (one that does not contain urea or ureic nitrogen). For terrariums with desert plants, it is best to use a cactus and succulent specific feed.

For open or partially open terrariums, mix the feed in the water at the recommended rate. For closed terrariums, mix at half strength – e.g. if the instructions recommend 10 ml per litre, it is best to use 5 ml per litre.

Use a feed with every other watering throughout the year.

Pruning

Some plants will need to be regularly pinched (or even pruned) to remain compact and in keeping with the display and the other plants.

Plants that will benefit from regular pinching/pruning:

Baby tears, crotons, nerve plants, golden clubmoss, inch plants, maidenhair vines, moon valley plants, rabbit foot ferns, Irish moss, Senecio, sphagnum moss, syngoniums, turtle vines.

Plants where pinching or pruning should be avoided:

Parlour palms, dracaenas, maidenhair ferns, peace lilies, strawberry begonia.

A partially open terrarium with overgrown plants (left), and after the plants were pruned. A top-up layer of decorative grit gives it a fresh look.

A partially open terrarium with a dragon tree and a peace lily, along with a couple of nerve plants for colour and contrast with the grit.

A partially open terrarium with a selection of plants around a piece of wood, which creates a woodland themed display.

A somewhat old-fashioned container (almost 40 years old) as a semi-open terrarium in two versions.

This is a classic version, with a variegated peperomia for height and a flowering kalanchoe for colour. Cork chippings provide a natural look.

Here the 'no-soil' effect is used (see p44), with a multicoloured decorative grit for a more contemporary style.

Advanced designs

The 'no-soil' effect

There are several ways you can make a terrarium so that you don't see either the clay pebbles at the bottom, or the compost. Instead, you can put it together so you only see grit (or layers of it) or any other material you find attractive like glass chippings or coloured sand. This technique can be used for all types of terrariums and the possibilities for artistic endeavours are almost endless.

There is one disadvantage to be aware of: watering will be trickier as you cannot use the colour of the pebbles or the compost as an indication.

Technique 1: Use a pot

For this method you will need a pot with good drainage which is smaller in diameter than the glass container, and when placed inside allows a small gap between it and the glass. Depending on the fit you may need to trim the top of the pot so it looks proportionate to the glass container. If the opening of the terrarium is too small for the pot to pass through you can cut off the bottom of the pot and make a cut on the side so it can be rolled together. It is not possible to use this technique with every glass container. It would be good to place a permeable membrane at the bottom (especially if you have cut off the bottom of the pot) to prevent soil coming out of the pot.

You will also need plenty of decorative gravel or grit, and/or any decorative material that you find visually attractive. Although this material will not come in direct contact with the compost (apart from the top layer) it is best to use materials that are clean and safe to use around plants. If you use sand, it is very important to use horticultural grade sand as it looks good and does not contain harmful chemicals.

How to put it together:

Place the pot inside the glass so there is some room between it and the glass. Depending on the fit you may need to trim the top of the pot so it looks in proportion to the glass container.

Fill the gap with layers of the decorative grit of your choice, almost to the rim of the pot.

Put some clay pebbles at the bottom of the pot and add activated carbon and soil as you would do in a normal terrarium. Place the plants, and finally cover with some of the grit you used for the layers.

❶ Cut a pot with good drainage to an appropriate size, relative to the glass container.

❷ Cut a permeable membrane to size and place it at the bottom of the pot to prevent soil coming out.

❸ Experiment to find the best combination of plants for the display, consider height, colour, and ground cover/depth.

❹ Add clay pebbles, activated carbon and potting mix in the pot, then place in the centre of the glass container. Pour varying depths of colourful sand layers around the pot with the help of a paper funnel.

❺ Place the chosen plants (slightly different selection here – you can always change your mind at the last minute!) and add a final layer of sand for top dressing. You can add a stone of a complimentary colour in the centre of the display to add interest.

Technique 2: Using card

Alternatively, you can use card to support the layers of the material next to the glass and remove it before you add the plants. With this technique you only need a piece of card, cut to the appropriate dimensions, and either stapled or taped together so that when placed inside the glass container there is a small gap between the paper and the glass. You can use grit, gravel, or horticultural sand. Either one type/colour or more to create a layered effect like the example below. By using sand, you can get an 'infinite desert' effect.

❶ Cut a piece of card to size and place it in the container, allowing a small gap all around it. Add clay pebbles and activated carbon in the centre to support the card. Alternate layers of sand are poured in the gap between the paper and the container.

❷ Pour repotting mix inside the card to support it against the weight of the sand. Pour more sand in varying depths in the gap and press down to eliminate any empty spaces within the sand.

❸ Once the desired height is achieved, remove the card slowly, and add more potting mix to fill the gap created by the removal of the card.

❹ A mixture of cacti and slow growing succulents creates a desert themed display. Complementary coloured slates are added to complete the look. The varying level of the sand adds interest.

Technique 3: Sticky sand

If you want to use sand for the 'no soil' effect, an alternative way to put the terrarium together is to stick the sand to the glass. As with the methods above, this is not possible with all containers (and very difficult with some) depending on the shape of the glass and whether you can put your hand in.

The easiest way to put it together is to do it gradually: build 2–3 cm of sand, add the clay pebbles and carbon, build another 2–3 cm, add the potting mix etc.

1 Moisten the sand adequately so it sticks well to the glass, and build it up around the glass to a thickness of 1–2 cm.

2 Add the clay pebbles and activated carbon.

3 Pour in the potting mix and place the plants.

4 Finally, add more sand to achieve an 'infinite desert' effect, with no soil in sight!

An alternative version of the same terrarium made with different colour sands.

An open terrarium with a peace lily, a couple of red nerve plants, and an inch plant for ground cover. It was put together using the pot technique *(see page 44)**, with three layers of colourful grit and glass chippings.*

An open terrarium with a mixture of cacti and succulents, put together using the pot technique. The multicoloured decorative grit and the cacti flowers create a busy display, and contrast nicely with the green cacti.

An open terrarium in the shape of a large glass, with three cacti planted very close together (they were grown this way in their original pot), and a few contrasting grit layers. It was created using the pot technique.

An open terrarium with a single cactus, put together using the pot technique. A dash of colour for a child's room.

The 'all-soil' effect

If you prefer to see only soil, there is a way to achieve this whilst incorporating a drainage layer so the terrarium can drain adequately between waterings. You can do this by altering the 'using a pot' or 'using a card' methods on pages 44 and 46.

You only need a piece of card, cut to the appropriate dimensions, and either stapled or taped together so that when placed inside the glass container there is a gap between the card and the glass. Alternatively, you can use a pot with good drainage which is smaller in diameter than the glass container, cut to an appropriate height (2–4 cm) which, when placed inside, allows a gap between it and the glass.

Simply place grit, gravel, or clay pebbles inside the card or the pot for the drainage layer, and add soil around.

Once you have placed the clay pebbles inside the card and the soil on the outside, remove the card and construct the terrarium as normal.

Using a pot will make it easier to contain the drainage layer (clay pebbles/grit) in the middle of the terrarium, especially if you use anything small grade.

A terrarium with moss

Putting together a moss terrarium is quite easy. It is best to use a closed container but an open or partially open one can also work with regular spraying and attention to watering.

Suitable mosses for terrariums include *Sphagnum* or peat moss which is very easy to source, mood moss (*Dicranum*), feather moss (*Hylocomium splendens*), horn calcareous moss (*Orthotrichum* spp.), and juniper haircap moss (*Polytrichum* spp.).

A moss terrarium is best kept outside, in a sheltered position, but a windowsill (especially when the window is open for a few hours every day) is also suitable. As discussed earlier, if the terrarium is closed, keep it away from direct sunlight, if it is open or partially open it can take a few hours sunlight every day especially in the winter.

For watering, you should use rainwater or deionised water. Closed terrariums will not need frequent watering, but open or partially-open moss terrariums will need a little water every week or so, and regular misting (again with rainwater or deionised water) to prevent the moss drying out.

How to put it together:
As most species lack substantial roots, you don't actually need any compost or drainage layer but you can use a thin layer of washed horticultural grit to minimise the risk or overwatering or having the moss sitting in too much water.

A simple moss terrarium. The peat moss sits on an inch-deep drainage layer of medium sized river pebbles. The arrangement of the slates make it an impressive display and very appealing to kids.

An alternative to a moss is a terrarium with 'baby tears' (see page 16). This plant – which, in the south of England, can be grown outdoors, too – spreads very quickly and is easy to look after. Like a moss terrarium, it can be kept outdoors or indoors.

A terrarium with carnivorous plants

Carnivorous plants can thrive in any type of terrarium, and the key to success is to keep the soil moist; their natural habitat is bogs and swamps. When watering, you need to use rainwater or deionised water to avoid the build-up of salts which can kill the plants.

A terrarium with carnivorous plants could be put together in a closed container with a removable lid, but its maintenance would be quite tricky as these plants need at least some direct sunlight. Although a closed terrarium would help the plants to retain moisture, you would have to open it regularly and place it in in direct sunlight to ensure healthy plant growth and for the plants to catch insects.

Hence, it is much better and easier to use an open or partially-open container and to place it somewhere it will receive least a couple of hours of direct sunlight throughout the year. An east- or west-facing windowsill would be ideal.

In May or June, once the nighttime temperatures are above 12°C, it is best to place the terrarium outside in a sheltered location, somewhere it will receive a couple of hours of sunlight. Keep an eye out for aphids, droughts, and sudden downpours. If you have a closed terrarium keep it open when outside.

How to put it together:

You can use most carnivorous plants such as bladderworts (*Utricularia* spp.), butterworts (*Pinguicula* spp.), Australian pitcher plants (*Cephalotus*), *Darlingtonia*, monkey traps (*Nepenthes*), pitcher plants (*Sarracenia*), sundews (*Drosera* spp.) and the ever-popular Venus fly traps (*Dionaea* spp.).

It is very important to use a specialist Carnivorous potting soil which contains no nutrients, and is slightly acidic which is what these plants need.

You can use sphagnum moss or stones around the carnivorous plants to help preserve moisture, and to mimic their natural habitat. If you use any stones or moss they need to be washed well before use to avoid excessive salts which can burn the roots.

An open terrarium with carnivorous plants and sphagnum moss. From left to right starting with the tallest plant: Drosera scorpiodes *(a large Pygmy sundew from Australia),* D. admirabilis *(a rosette-forming sundew) and* D. capensis *'Crested'.*

An open terrarium with a single carnivorous plant (Drosera capensis 'Crested') and sphagnum moss for ground cover.

An open terrarium with a collection of carnivorous plants and sphagnum moss. From left to right, starting from the plant at the centre back: Nepenthes gaya (a highland hybrid), Nepenthes lowii x Nepenthes ventricose (another highland hybrid), Pinguicula Guatemala (an ideal indoor butterwort with pink flowers, loves whiteflies), Pinguicula x Wesser (an easy-to-grow butterwort with pink flowers).

A terrarium with air plants

Although strictly speaking not a terrarium, making a display with air plants in a glass container is easy and highly decorative.

Apart from the air plants (*Tillandsia* spp.) you will need some decorative grit, gravel, sand, as well as some rocks, stones, wood or any other natural items you like, such as seashells. It is best to use a partially open, or fully open, glass container.

Air plants prefer bright light, and can take some direct sun. Too little light can cause air plants to suddenly fail and die, so place the display in a bright spot.

How to put it together:

Add a 'base layer' such as sand, or gravel to the bottom of the terrarium, and on top place any other items you want. Finally, place the air plants. Using different types and sizes of air plants adds interest to the display. Some air plants are fine leaved and others coarser in texture, so there are plenty of options for variation. One or two for a more minimal look... or as many as you can fit for a jungle effect.

Air plant care

Watering air plants is easy. Once a week, remove the air plants from the glass container, gather them in a large bowl or sink, and soak them in water for a couple of hours. Do this by completely covering the plant with room temperature tap or filtered water. Rain or aquarium water work well too. Let them drain upside down on a towel. Air plants are prone to rot if water is allowed to pool in their leaves, so when removing the plants from the water turn them upside down, gently shake and allow them to dry out almost completely before placing them back into the display pot or surface. Morning immersions are better for the plants than evening ones.

To keep your plants healthy, feed using a low-strength fertiliser such as Orchid Focus Grow. Include in the water when immersing, at the recommended rate for orchids. Use with every other watering, throughout the year. For best results mist them regularly with a quality mist such as Air Plant Myst.

A semi open terrarium with a deep base of different layers of decorative grit for added interest and variation.

An open terrarium with air plants. A simple glass bowl with a selection of stones, wood and air plants.

A collection of colourful pebbles, driftwood and stone ornaments, make this semi-open air plant terrarium highly decorative.

A small, open terrarium in a cube-shaped container, made with the card technique. A combination of cacti, stones and pine wood makes for an interesting, desert themed display.

'Non-terrarium' terrariums

The principle and technique of terrarium-making discussed in this book can be applied to non-glass containers. Ornamental pots, containers of any size (even large coffee cups) can be used to make an attractive display. As with glass containers, add a thin layer of clay pebbles, some activated charcoal and potting mix. You can use any plant as these non-transparent containers are the equivalent of an open terrarium.

A large coffee cup, with a flowering cactus. The drainage layer at the bottom will ensure the substrate drains adequately.

An indoor planter with no drainage, planted with cacti. Six months after the initial planting, the plants are thriving.

A large coffee cup with a single cactus a year after its creation. It looks as good as the day it was made.

An open terrarium in a square acrylic container. Three Banksia seed pods of varying heights complement the dragon trees and the fittonia in the front.

A mini Chamaedora palm provides height in a green colour-based terrarium arrangement, with a splash of colour provided by a mini nicotiana plant.

Terrariums with cacti or succulents in geometrical shapes are very popular. They do not need frequent watering, which helps to keep the metal frame free from oxidation. As the plants grow very slowly, they last for long time without looking overgrown. Adding stones or decorative wood pieces enhances the displays and adds interest.

Common questions and answers

Q: I can see some green growth on the inside of the glass. What is it?

This is very likely to be algae. It can occur inside the glass of a closed terrarium, or by the grit, compost, or even drainage layer especially on the side towards the light. Algae are not harmful to the terrarium; it is simply a natural part of its ecosystem.

If, however, you do not like the way it looks, you can wipe it away with a clean cloth. Removing algae from around the potting compost and drainage layer is trickier. One way is to use a big spoon or spatula and move the compost back, taking care not to disturb the plants. To prevent algae in the first place, keep the glass clean (see below) and the terrarium on the dry side.

If there is at least some humidity and light, algae can grow almost anywhere – even in a desert terrarium. Keeping the terrarium on the dry side will keep its growth in check.

Q: Shall I clean the glass of my terrarium? If so, how?

Yes, this is a good idea for closed or partially-open terrariums where the glass surrounds the plants. Regular cleaning will ensure the plants receive as much light as possible and grow to their full potential.

It is best to simply use water when cleaning a terrarium. Cleaning detergent falling on the surface of the terrarium can change the pH value in the compost and make it acidic. This will damage the plants and upset the delicate balance inside your closed ecosystem.

Q: My terrarium is not looking great, with some overgrown plants and some dead ones. What can I do?

Every few months you can 'renovate' your mini indoor garden, just as you would with an outside garden. Replace any plants that do not look great (no need to allow a period before adding new plants, if there is no suspicion of disease) and maybe add a new layer of decorative grit for a fresh look.

A mature and somewhat neglected terrarium, with a couple of leggy, overgrown nerve plants in the front. Not looking its best.

The dead leaves of the palm have been removed, the nerve plants replaced with a polka dot plant, and two different grits used for top dressing. As good as new!

Q: A plant in my terrarium has died. What am I to do?

It can sometimes happen that one or two plants die soon after you make the terrarium due to excessive damage to their root systems or possibly because of root rot. If this happens, remove them, wait a week or so (no watering during this week) and replace with a similar plant.

If some of the plants die long after the terrarium is established, you need to review the overall environment. The most common reason for plants dying in terrariums is overwatering. Remove the dead plants and any rotten leaves (to prevent spread of any disease), and after a week or so add new plants.

Q: My plants have black leaves? What can I do?

If some leaves inside the terrarium are black (and especially soggy) it is very likely that the terrarium is receiving too little light and is kept very moist. This can occur with closed terrariums where the leaves touch the glass. Remove all the black leaves, open the lid (if the terrarium has one) and if possible, move to a location with better aeration. Reduce future waterings to prevent this from happening again.

A pear-shaped, closed terrarium, with a collection of ferns and colourful gravel for contrast and added interest. Condensation is a feature of closed terrariums. For this terrarium, it would be better if the depth of the potting mix was lower, so the leaves of the ferns do not touch the glass. If they do, they can turn black.

Q: My plants have some yellow (or dried or dead) leaves. What can I do?

If there is one yellow leaf at the bottom of the plant, it is probably natural, just remove it. If, however, there are a few, and the soil is quite wet, it may indicate root rot. If the top leaves become yellow, perhaps with some brown spots, it is likely they have been damaged by direct sunlight, so move the terrarium to a different location away from direct sun – but as bright as possible for maximum plant growth. Another possible cause of yellowing (and the most likely cause of dried or dead leaves) is very dry soil. Check the soil. Is it light brown? Does the terrarium feel light? If so, the dryness is causing the yellow leaves, in which case you need to adjust the frequency of watering.

Q: My terrarium has turned into an overgrown jungle. What shall I do?

Many people like the overgrown jungle effect! But apart from terrariums with cacti and succulents, most terrariums will eventually take over the container, especially if it is closed. If pinching or pruning cannot solve the problem because the plants are not pinchable or have reached a certain size, you can remove the plants to normal pots for further growing, remove the soil and gravel, give the glass a good clean with soapy water and start all over again with a new terrarium.

Bear in mind, the more plants you place in the terrarium and the bigger they are, the quicker it will reach the overgrown jungle stage.

Two examples of overgrown displays. The apple (left) is looking very overgrown and is probably ready for replanting, whereas the large bottle (right) has a few more months in it.

Q: Small black flies are hovering around my terrarium. What shall I do?

These are likely to be fungus gnats (Sciaridae), also known as house plant flies or sciarid flies. They are very small and slender, mosquito-like flies. Unless you keep your terrarium very wet, they would only be likely to appear if you used a repotting mix which contains the eggs already. They hatch when in warm conditions. Gnats and their larvae cause little or no harm to plants. They should disperse if you open the windows, and you can use yellow sticky traps to attract the adults. Allow the compost to dry out between waterings to minimise any chance of the flies laying eggs. Fungus gnat eggs and larvae require moist soil and soon die if they dry out. If your terrarium does not have a layer of decorative grit, it would be very helpful if you cover its surface with a 1cm-thick layer of gravel, grit or ornamental glass pebbles. This will stop house plant flies from being able to lay their eggs. The above also applies to normal houseplants.

Q: What can I do to prevent pests?

Pests are not very common but it is good to inspect your terrarium (and all your houseplants) carefully at regular intervals, especially in the spring. If you spot any insects or disease symptoms, isolate, and treat the plants or your terrarium immediately to prevent other plants in the house getting infected.

If you do get a pest infestation, you can either use a 'systemic' or a 'contact' insecticide. A systemic insecticide gets into the 'system' of the plant; the insects suck the plant sap and die. It is effective, but highly toxic.

Contact insecticides cover the bugs in a fatty substance which suffocates them. They are normally safe to use inside the home, even if you have pets or children. You will need to spray all the plants fully to make sure you reach all the bugs. As contact insecticides do not normally kill eggs, you will need to spray the plants well at least four times (once every four days).

In any case, before you spray, use a cotton bud dipped in alcohol to physically remove as many of the pests as you can, including any eggs you can see. Look between any crevices under the leaves and remove any leaves that may house any pests.

Clean the glass with soapy water, and the area around the terrarium with dilute bleach. Always follow the instructions on the product label.

Spider mites can sometimes affect open or partially open terrariums in hot, dry weather. Regular misting will minimise any potential problems.

Q: How can I prevent diseases?

Root rot (*Phytophthora spp.*) is the most common disease. It starts with yellowing lower leaves and poor growth (due to damaged roots) and ends with the death of the plant. 'Mushy' roots are normally caused by root rot. It can occur when the terrarium is over watered. It is near impossible to cure it. The best prevention is correct watering and to avoid any damage to the roots.

Grey mould or botrytis (*Botrytis cinerea*) can occur in closed or partially open terrariums where humidity can build up. It can occur if you have used the wrong plants for a closed terrarium, when there is excess moisture (such as in a closed terrarium), in low light conditions, and when rotten debris is allowed to remain in the terrarium. It can spread very quickly. Open the lid of closed terrariums regularly (if possible) to allow some air circulation, and always remove any dead leaves from the terrarium.

Q: What is causing white 'threads' on the leaves, white fluffy insects in the plant crevices or a cotton wool-like mass on some plants of my terrarium?

The most likely reason is that the terrarium is infected with mealybugs. This is rare, but it can happen.

There are many types of mealybug. These sap-sucking insects are white and appear fluffy, like cotton wool, and are 1–5 mm in size. Their activity and growth depend on the temperature – the higher the temperature, the faster they multiply. Mealybugs suck sap from the plant, causing distortion, yellowing and loss of leaves. They produce honeydew that can become infected with sooty mould. Mealybugs can enter the home from outside, come from other houseplants, or they may already be on the plant or in the growing medium when you buy it (but may not be visible or very active due to the temperature). The first sign of their presence is a cotton wool-like mass on the leaves or other soft parts of the plant. These are mealybug eggs, and if you take no action, you will soon see live nymphs appear. Mealybugs often hide in the crevices of plants where the leaves meet the stem. They can also hide in the grit, decorations, or any other nooks and crannies within the terrarium.

Mealybugs on a Dracaena

Remove the threads and any insects with a cotton bud dipped in alcohol and wipe the leaves clean regularly to prevent an infestation. See below for more information on prevention and treatment.

Q: My terrarium is not looking great

This is a one year old terrarium kept in very low light conditions (hence the leggy plants), with no regular pinching (so one of the nerve plants got very leggy). It has been allowed to dry too much, which explains the yellow tips of the peace lily leaves. It is salvable if the nerve plant is replaced, moved to brighter conditions and some more decorative added. It is however, worth considering moving the peace lily to a normal pot and start all over again with a new display.

Q: What are these small bright yellow little balls in the soil? What can I do?

This is fungal growth. Specifically, these are the sclerotia (a compact mass of hardened fungal mycelium containing food reserves) of *Leucocoprinus birnbaumii*, a species of gilled mushroom. This fungus is saprotrophic, which means it feeds on dead organic matter and is harmless to plants. Its presence may even improve the quality of the soil it as it can help to break down organic matter and provide nutrients that the plants require.

L. birnbaumii is known as the 'plant pot dapperling' or 'flowerpot parasol' and it is common in the tropics and subtropics. In temperate regions, it occurs in greenhouses and potting soil, hence its common names. For potted plants and terrariums, it is likely that the spores of the fungus were in the coir (coco fibre), which normally originates in India or Sri Lanka, used in the potting mix. It is toxic if consumed.

It is unlikely the fungus will develop any mushrooms unless the soil is kept very wet. Even if it does, the mushrooms can be quite attractive. So, one option is to leave it as it is especially if it is out of reach of any pets or children.

It is actually pretty difficult to remove from the soil so the other option is to dispose of the soil and plants, and wash the glass container very well.

The appearance of this fungus has remained the same for over a year, as the terrarium has been kept not too wet and the decorative grit at the top prevents further spread.

Q: After I pinched my plant, the new leaves have grown much smaller. Have I done anything wrong?

Pinching prevents leggy growth and makes plants bushier but it can have this effect on many plants, especially if the light is not ideal and/or the temperature relatively high.

The leaves will grow bigger in time but will not reach the size of the old ones. If smaller leaves are not desired, the only option is to avoid pinching.

The best way to ensure that plants do not grow leggy without pinching is to place the terrarium in very bright – but indirect – light whilst avoiding high temperatures.

Peperomias will develop smaller leaves after pinching out.

Q: The plants inside my terrarium are leaning towards one side. Why?
Or: **The plants inside my terrarium are leggy. Why? What can I do?**

The reason for both is insufficient light. It can happen with all houseplants but is even more common with terrariums as glass reduces the available light even further. To avoid the problem occurring in the first place, use plants that require low light and prune or pinch them regularly. If you get leggy plants the best thing to do is to place the terrarium in a brighter position and prune or tip the plants to encourage bushy growth.

Q: The new leaves of my variegated croton lack any variegation? Why? What can I do?

Again, the culprit is light, and it sometimes happens with variegated plants such as crotons, variegated dragon trees etc. Placing the plant in a brighter position will not make these leaves become variegated, but it is likely that further new ones will be.

Plants for terrariums

Closed terrariums

The plants listed below will do well in a closed terrarium as they require high humidity. They will also do well in a partially or fully open terrarium, especially if misted regularly.

Common name	Latin name	Comments
Irish moss or green moss	*Sagina subulata*	Resembles moss, great for ground cover.
Baby Tears	*Soleirolia species or Helexine species*	Great ground cover. Green or variegated.
Maidenhair Ferns	*Adiantum spp.*	Light green leaves with smooth black stalks.
Rabbit Foot Ferns	*Davallia fejeensis*	Beautiful leaves.
Earth Star	*Cryptanthus bivittatus*	Adds colour and texture.
Lemon Button Fern	*Nephrolepis cordifolia*	Very popular, easy to care for.
Button Fern	*Pellaea rotundifolia*	Adds texture, low growing.
Fluffy Ruffles Fern	*Nephrolepis exaltata*	Graceful, arching green fronds.
Silver Ribbon Fern	*Pteris cretica*	Clump-forming, with light green fronds.
Asparagus Fern	*Plumosa nanus*	Very architectural plant, ideal to add height.
Indian Fern	*Arachnoides simplicior*	A slow-growing fern bearing thick, glossy, broadly-triangular, dark green fronds.
Peacock Fern	*Selaginella uncinata*	With iridescent blues and greens, very quick growing.
Maidenhair Vine	*Meuhlenbeckia complexa*	Dark green leaves, climbing habit.
Creeping Fig	*Ficus pumila*	Tiny bubbled variegated leaves. Trailing habit.
Silver Sparkle	*Pilea glauca*	With tiny, rounded, silvery grey-green leaves. Trailing habit.
String of Turtles	*Peperomia prostrata*	Compact growth, trailing habit. Red stems bearing circular leaves with dark green markings.
Silver Sprinkles	*Pilea glauca*	Low growing, with very small, silver-blue leaves.
Dwarf Arrowhead Vine	*Syngonium podophyllum*	Trailing habit, arrow-shaped leaves.
Aluminium Plant	*Pilea cadierei*	Obovate leaves marked with silver patches.
Moon Valley Plant	*Pilea mollis*	Thick, textured leaves with fine hairs. Very eye-catching.
Nerve Plant	*Fittonia albivenis*	They are great for colour. Striking leaf pattern, with white or pink veining. Comes in many varieties.
Polka Dot Plant	*Hypoestes phyllostachya*	These are very colourful and often confused with nerve plants. They are very similar, but they can be distinguished by their veins: Hypoestes has green veins; nerve plants have pink or white veins. Both come in many varieties.
Dragon Tree	*Dracaena species*	Slow growing, ideal for adding height in small containers. Green or variagated.

Inch Plants	*Tradescantia species*	Great for ground cover, trailing habit.
Variegated Peperomia	*Peperomia Obtusifolia 'variagata'*	Upright and spreading with leathery, bright green leaves with wide yellow-green margins.
Radiator Plant	*Peperomia caperata*	Striking red undersides and deeply grooved glossy leaves.
'Red Log' Radiator Plant	*Peperomia verticilata 'Red Log'*	Small, thick leaves which are deep green on top and vibrant red underneath. Compact growth.
Strawberry Begonia	*Saxifraga sarmentosa*	Hairy dark green leaves with silvery veins (above, reddish beneath).

Partially open or open terrariums

Any small plant will do well in an open or partially open terrarium, the only limitation being the size of the plant and possibly how fast it grows. Cacti and succulents are great for fully open terrariums or partially open terrariums with a large opening, but they should not be placed in a closed terrarium as the high humidity is likely to cause root rot.

Common name	**Latin name**	**Comments**
Parlour Palm	*Chamaedorea elegans*	Excellent for height with an exotic feel.
Croton	*Codiaeum variegatum*	Can be used for height, adds colour.
Golden Clubmoss	*Selaginella kraussiana*	Ground-hugging, with a distinctive yellow colouring.
Mountain Fire	*Senecio cephalophorus*	Amazing silver leaves, good for height.
Turtle Vines	*Callisia repens*	Great for ground cover. Variegated or green leaves.
Missionary Plant	*Pilea peperomioides*	Has fleshy, rounded, long-stalked mid-green leaves.
Golden Pothos	*Epipremnum aureum*	Glossy bright green ovate leaves.
Peace Lily	*Spathiphyllum wallisii*	Great for height, easy to flower.

Cacti and succulents:

Aloes	*Aloe spp.*	Easy to grow, many varieties.
Panda Plant	*Kalanchoe tomentosa*	Thick, soft, furry leaves.
Bunny Ears cactus	*Opuntia microdasys*	Unique looking.
Burro's Tail	*Sedum morganianum burritum*	Succulent with trailing stems and blue-green leaves.
Jade Plant	*Crassula ovata*	Succulent. Great for height.
Mount Everest Plant	*Ledebouria spp.*	Beautiful, patterned leaves.
Zebra cactus	*Haworthiopsis attenuata*	Small succulent, easy to propagate.
String of Pearls	*Senecio rowleyanus*	Very distinctive, trailing habit.
Snake Plant	*Sansevieria trifasciata*	Difficult to kill. Great for height.
Living Stones	*Lithops spp.*	Good for ground cover, very slow growing.
Houseleek	*Sempervivum spp.*	Forms a mat, green or silver leaves.
Elephant Bush	*Portulacaria afra*	Small leaves, green or variegated. Excellent for ground cover.
Barrel cactus	*Rebutia heliosa*	Has white spines in contrast with dark green foliage.
Hedgehog cactus	*Echinocereus reichenbachii*	Good for height, very distinctive.
Woolly Nipple cactus	*Mammillaria spp.*	Slow growing and barrel-like.

Recommended products

After extensive research I strongly recommend the following products. I have been involved in their development and in my experience, they give consistently good results.

Houseplant Focus

Suitable for all indoor houseplants. Houseplant Focus will provide all the necessary nutrients needed by the plants to compensate for the declining fertility of the compost. It is manufactured to the highest standards from pure mineral salts and rich organic nutrients.

Organic Houseplant Focus

This is the organic option for thriving terrariums, naturally. Please note that it is likely to discolour very light coloured decorative grit.

Cactus & Succulent Focus

Balanced nutrient solution for cacti and succulents, or terrariums with cacti or terrariums. It contains all the necessary macro- and micro-nutrients, as well as organic plant extracts such as humic and fulvic acids.

Organic Cactus & Succulent Focus

The organic option for all cacti and succulents. Ideal for terrariums with cacti or succulents. Please note that it is likely to discolour very light coloured decorative grit.

Air Plant Myst

The ideal way to feed air plants and provide them with humidity and all the necessary nutrients for healthy growth. Ready to use.

Terrarium Focus Repotting Mix

Ideal for both closed and open terrariums.

Cactus and Succulent Focus Repotting Mix

Designed for best results with the widest range of cacti and succulents. It also contains a balanced range of nutrients to support growth for up to two months.

Houseplant Focus Repotting Mix

A good mix for terrariums with foliage plants.

Clay pebbles

Medium grade pebbles (8–16 mm), the ideal material for the drainage layer in terrariums.

Activated Carbon

Lightweight and highly absorbent, it has oxygen added to increase porosity and surface area.

SB Plant Invigorator

A great contact insecticide for use with all plants. It will control most common houseplant pests including mealybugs, spider mites, whitefly and aphids.

From the same author:

An authoritative and detailed guide to caring for orchids in the home – the result of experience, continuous experimentation and extensive research by expert authors. All common types of orchids are covered. The only book you need when growing orchids at home.